Dear Parents and Educators,

Welcome to Penguin Young Readers! As parents and educators, you know that each child develops at their own pace—in terms of speech, critical thinking, and, of course, reading. Penguin Young Readers recognizes this fact. As a result, each Penguin Young Readers book is assigned a traditional easy-to-read level (1–4) as well as an F&P Text Level (A–R). Both of these systems will help you choose the right book for your child. Please refer to the back of each book for specific leveling information. Penguin Young Readers features esteemed authors and illustrators, stories about favorite characters, fascinating nonfiction, and more!

A World of Dancers

LEVEL **4**

F&P TEXT LEVEL **P**

This book is perfect for a **Fluent Reader** who:
- can read the text quickly with minimal effort;
- has good comprehension skills;
- can self-correct (can recognize when something doesn't sound right); and
- can read aloud smoothly and with expression.

Here are some **activities** you can do during and after reading this book:
- Nonfiction: Nonfiction books deal with facts and events that are real. Talk about the elements of nonfiction. Then, on a separate sheet of paper, write down the facts you learned about the following types of dances: dance ceremonies, folk dances, and performance dances.
- Creative Writing: Pretend you are performing in a talent show at your school. Write a paragraph about which sort of dance you would like to perform and why.

Remember, sharing the love of reading with a child is the best gift you can give!

*This book has been officially leveled by using the F&P Text Level Gradient™ leveling system.

For my Nia dance tribe around the world,
but especially in Richmond, Virginia:
Thank you for seeing me and for letting
yourself be seen—GLC

PENGUIN YOUNG READERS
An imprint of Penguin Random House LLC, New York

First published in the United States of America by Penguin Young Readers,
an imprint of Penguin Random House LLC, New York, 2023

Photo credits: used throughout: (photo frame) happyfoto/E+/Getty Images; cover, 3: NinaHenry/
iStock/Getty Images; 4: photosvit/iStock/Getty Images; 5: JackF/iStock/Getty Images; 6–7: wind-moon/
iStock Editorial/Getty Images; 8: alantobey/iStock/Getty Images; 9: alantobey/E+/Getty Images; 10:
Mike Powell/The Image Bank/Getty Images; 11: LazingBee/iStock Unreleased/Getty Images; 12:
Jupiterimages/The Image Bank/Getty Images; 13: FatCamera/E+/Getty Images; 14: Global_Pics/E+/
Getty Images; 15: PeopleImages/iStock/Getty Images; 16: UniversalImagesGroup/Universal Images
Group Editorial/Getty Images; 17: RJ Sangosti/Denver Post/Getty Images; 18: mycan/iStock/Getty
Images; 19: uchar/E+/Getty Images; 20: DEA/G. DAGLI ORTI/De Agostini/De Agostini Editorial/Getty
Images; 21: Jane Tregelles/Alamy Stock Photo; 22: PaulaConnelly/E+/Getty Images; 23: AnnSteer/
E+/Getty Images; 24: Gannet77/E+/Getty Images; 25: clu/DigitalVision Vectors/Getty Images;
26–27: Vyacheslav Madiyevskyy/Ukrinform/Future Publishing/Getty Images; 28: DEA/BIBLIOTECA
AMBROSIANA/De Agostini/De Agostini Editorial/Getty Images; 29: Horst Mahr/imageBROKER/
Alamy Stock Photo; 30: Westend61/Getty Images; 31: (top) Simone Hogan/iStock/Getty Images,
(bottom) BraneBoi/E+/Getty Images; 32: Göran Algård Collection/Historisk Bildbyrå/Mustang media/
Heritage Images/Heritage Image Partnership Ltd./Alamy Stock Photo; 33: clu/DigitalVision Vectors/
Getty Images; 34: JAPAN POOL/AFP/Getty Images; 35: Linda Vartoogian/Archive Photos/Getty
Images; 36: duncan1890/DigitalVision Vectors/Getty Images; 37: PeopleImages/iStock/Getty Images;
38: hadynyah/E+/Getty Images; 39: joakimbkk/iStock/Getty Images; 40: IndiaPix/IndiaPicture/Getty
Images; 41: Tibor Bognar/The Image Bank Unreleased/Getty Images; 42–43: Gabriel Perez/Moment
Open/Getty Images; 44: artJazz/iStock/Getty Images; 45: (top) Vanish_Point/iStock/Getty Images,
(bottom) nensuria/iStock/Getty Images; 46–47: (background) adamkaz/E+/Getty Images; 47: (inset)
joshblake/E+/Getty Images; 48: FatCamera/iStock/Getty Images

Visit us online at penguinrandomhouse.com.

Library of Congress Cataloging-in-Publication Data is available.

Manufactured in China

ISBN 9780593384022 (pbk)   10 9 8 7 6 5 4 3 2 1 WKT
ISBN 9780593384039 (hc)   10 9 8 7 6 5 4 3 2   WKT

PENGUIN YOUNG READERS

LEVEL
4
FLUENT
READER

A WORLD OF DANCERS

by
Ginjer L. Clarke

People all around the world love to dance. They dress up and move their bodies to music or sounds. They dance in groups, pairs, and alone. Some dances are used to celebrate. Other dances help people tell stories, express their feelings, and connect with one another.

Dancing is important in all places and cultures and for people of all ages. It is also a lot of fun! Let's take a tour around the globe to learn about a world of dancers.

Dance Ceremonies

Ceremonies are events that happen around big life moments. Some cultures use dances as part of ceremonies for weddings, funerals, and festivals.

The dragon dance celebrates the Lunar New Year to bring good luck.

Boom! Boom! A drummer and dancers wind their way through the streets. Crowds cheer them on.

These Chinese dancers hold up a long, colorful dragon puppet on poles. They wear gold, green, and red costumes to match the dragon. They leap and turn to move the dragon up, down, and around. *Swoop!* The dragon looks as if it can really fly!

8

The Dogon people in Mali also dance dressed as animals. They wear painted masks that look like birds, snakes, and antelope. Some dancers even walk on tall stilts to look like long-legged water birds!

Rattle! The masked dancers shake their shell-and-grass costumes. *Clang! Clang!* Cowbells and drums are played. The dancers circle around a pole.

This African dance honors the spirits of tribe members who have died. The ceremony is only held about every twelve years, but it lasts for up to five days!

One famous dance is a battle ceremony. The Māori (say: MOU-ree) people of New Zealand perform the haka war dance. This dance makes their muscles strong, brings them together as a group, and can even scare their enemies.

Stomp! The haka dancers stamp their feet, slap their legs, and wave their hands. They make a lot of noise. *Shout! Shout!* They open their eyes wide and stick their tongues out. Many Māori people also have face tattoos, which may make them look even fiercer.

People do gentler dances on the islands of Hawaii. Hula dances used to be part of ceremonies to honor Hawaiian gods. These dances tell stories about nature and feelings.

Swish! The hula dancers move side to side and sway their skirts. They use arm and hand motions that look like rain, waves, flowers, and trees.

The dancers used to speak poems out loud as they moved to drums. Now hula dances often use guitar and ukulele music, too. *Strum! Strum!*

Samba is a fast, bouncy dance that celebrates life. Samba dance teams compete for prizes at the yearly parade called Carnival in Brazil.

La! La! La! The costumed dancers move and sing to loud music. They also ride on huge parade floats.

The solo samba dancers wear sparkly costumes and lots of flashy feathers. The dancers shake and flap like fancy birds. *Wiggle! Wiggle!*

A powwow is also partly a dance contest. Native American tribes from all over North America gather to show their traditions through dance. Some dances honor animals such as deer. Other dances celebrate skills such as pottery-making.

Zuni pottery dance

Fancy
dance

Fancy dances show a dancer's talent.
Fancy dancers wear beaded costumes
and headdresses made of feathers. "Hey-
ya-ya-ya!" Singers and drummers set the
beat for the dancers. *Jingle! Jangle!* Bells
on the dancers' legs and ankles keep the
beat as they spin and jump.

Swirl! Twirl! Whirling dervish dancers spin around in circles—sometimes for hours! The dervishes are members of a Muslim group in Turkey. They are dancing as part of a ceremony to honor their god.

Whoosh! The dervishes whirl faster, with their arms spread out. Their long gowns make circles around them. The dervishes represent planets turning. Their leader in the center is the sun. This spinning is meant to help the dervishes go into a dreamlike state.

Folk Dances

Folk dances were used by people long ago to learn to cooperate. This helped them work together. Folk dancing also gave people pride in their culture.

Ancient Greeks danced in circles. They believed dancing was a gift from the gods. The Greeks left clues about dancing in their paintings, sculptures, and pottery.

Greek people still do folk dances in circles. They hold hands and move together. The lead dancer holds a scarf and does harder steps. *Wheee!* The dancers go faster. "Opa!" They shout with joy.

Morris folk dancing began in England in the 1400s to celebrate the change of seasons. Morris dancers today compete as groups of neighbors to create team spirit.

Each team usually dresses in matching white shirts, straw hats with flowers, and bright sashes. *Ring! Ring!* The dancers shake bells on their legs and shoes as they step and hop. They wave magic wands to bring luck. *Ta-da!* They also use sticks, scarves, and even swords as they dance.

Swords can be dangerous! But Highland folk dancing in Scotland includes a special sword dance. This dance was first done in the 1500s by Scottish warriors. They had to prove to their war chief that they were strong and quick.

The swords are placed on the ground in an X shape. *Wah! Wah!* The bagpipes begin to wail. The Highland dancers raise their arms. They step all around the swords. *Leap!* They dance on their toes, so they never touch the swords!

The national dance of Ukraine is the hopak. This word means "to jump." Hopak dancers jump a lot! The hopak was a way for soldiers to show off their skills, just like in the Scottish sword dance.

Hop! The hopak dancers do squatting kicks, spinning turns, and jumping splits. "Hup! Hup!" They also shout as they leap into the air. The dancers who jump the highest become famous.

The quadrille (say: kwa-DRILL) dance has an interesting history. It was first danced in the royal courts of France in the 1700s. Then it became popular in England and on several Caribbean islands, such as Jamaica, when some English people moved there and took over. The enslaved African people in

Jamaica learned the dance and added their own style. Eventually the quadrille became a fun folk dance for the free Jamaican people.

Hello! Four couples in matching outfits stand in a square shape and bow to each other. Let's go! They link arms, stepping and turning together in different patterns.

In the United States, quadrille is now called square dancing. It is even the official dance of more than 20 states.

Polka is another folk dance that started in one country and moved to another. Polka music and dancing began in the 1800s in Bohemia. Then many people from this area in Europe moved to Mexico to find work. They brought the polka with them.

Squeeze! Musicians play polka on the accordion—a small, piano-like instrument that they squeeze. Couples dance to the fast, cheerful 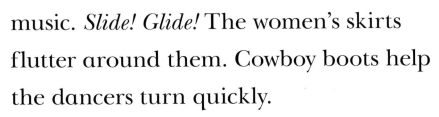 music. *Slide! Glide!* The women's skirts flutter around them. Cowboy boots help the dancers turn quickly.

The tarantella (say: TARE-an-tell-uh) is a superfast dance with an odd story. People in Italy in the 1500s were sometimes bitten by tarantulas.

They were told to do a wild dance to cure themselves of the tarantula's venom. The high-energy dance was later called the tarantella, or spider dance.

Italian couples still dance the tarantella for fun. *Kick!* The men move their legs in spiderlike motions. *Shake! Shake!* The women play tambourines—small drums with metal disks that jingle—to keep the beat.

Performance Dances

Some dances take so much skill and practice that dancers train a long time to do them. These dancers perform for audiences and tell stories as art.

Kabuki (say: kuh-BOO-kee) dancers in Japan train in music, acting, and martial arts. They use super-slow moves to tell stories about heroes and villains. Sometimes a dancer has to hold one pose for an hour!

Shhh! Kabuki dancers wear only white socks on their feet so they can move quietly. But they do not stay quiet for long. *Ha! Ya!* They shout as they dance.

Many ballet dancers begin training as young as three years old to learn the difficult moves. Female ballet dancers, or ballerinas, wore long skirts and shoes with heels before the 1700s. Then one famous dancer created a costume with a short, stiff skirt called a tutu. She also wore soft, flat slippers so she could jump better. Later, another ballerina danced on the tips of her toes in hard slippers called pointe shoes. These costumes are still worn by ballerinas today!

Dancers in Cambodia also train from a young age to learn Khmer (say: kuh-MEHR) classical dance. They do not dress like ballerinas. But Khmer classical dancers work just as hard to learn difficult moves.

Twist! Khmer classical dancers make shapes with their bodies. The shapes tell adventure stories. In one famous type of classical dance, each dancer plays one of four roles: a man, woman, giant, or monkey.

The dancers keep their faces calm, and sometimes they wear masks. They move their hands and arms to look like trees, flowers, waves, and even snakes. *Hiss!*

The name *bharatanatyam* (say: buh-HA-ruh-ta-NOT-yum) comes from four Indian words that mean "feelings," "song," "movement," and "drama." This dance tells stories about Hindu gods through the dancers' feelings and movements.

Tinkle! Tinkle! Bharatanatyam dancers wear tiny bells on their ankles that make music as the dancers move. *Look!* The dancers open their eyes wide and raise their eyebrows to show surprise. Their hands and feet are painted with red dye to show off their poses.

Korean fan dancing centers around the large fans the dancers hold. The dancers wear long dresses that cover their feet. *Float!* It looks as if they are moving without touching the floor.

Many fan dances begin with the dancers covering their faces with the

fans. Then the dancers start moving
slowly, like they are just waking up.
Flip! Flap! The dancers move their fans
together into shapes that look like
wings, flowers, trees, water, and even
sea creatures.

Flamenco dancers in Spain sometimes use large fans in their dance, too. But they dance alone or in couples. And they dance fast and loud!

Flick! A female flamenco dancer flutters her dress. She claps her hands to guitar music. She also keeps the beat with castanets—round instruments played with her fingers. *Click! Clack!*

The
dancer
stomps
her feet.
She even
has tiny nail
heads on the
bottom of her shoes
to make extra noise! She yells, "Olé!" at
the end of the dance.

Tap dance also uses noisy shoes and fast feet. Tap is sometimes called America's national dance because it began in the United States. It was created by enslaved people to share information with each other when they were not allowed to talk while working.

Tippity-tap! Tap shoes have metal plates on the toes and heels. Dancers use lots of moves to make fun patterns. *Sliiide!* Tap dancers today are still inventing new steps to make their dances even more interesting.

Dancing is great for your body and brain. It can even make you happier! Maybe you take dance lessons or dance with friends or on your own. Any way you dance is the right way—wherever you live in the world. Get moving and have fun!